The Lord's

Army

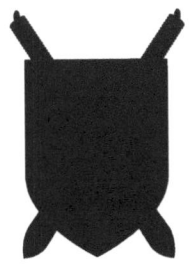

TAS

ISBN: 978-1-960853-52-3

Printing in USA

Liberation's Publishing LLC
501 7th St. N Suite 4 – Columbus, MS. 39701

Dedicated to God's People.

The Lord's Army

CONTENTS

.

INTRODUCTION

This fictional tale is written to inspire, to unite, and to layout a foundation. Hopefully, the previous two novels in this four-part series have opened your eyes to fundamental problems in our world. If they have, you must've come to the realization that it's up to us to fix what's gone wrong, as the ones in whom we've entrusted that job to have utterly failed. The deceit of riches and power have corrupted the souls of the shepherds of the world; therefore, we're left with no choice. Our strength lies in our numbers, but in order to unite you must also believe that there can be something better than what now exists, and you must have faith in the unseen. My goal through writing is to help you along the path that leads to all the aforementioned. As always, I hope you enjoy. I hope you are enlightened, and I hope you believe.

The Lord's Army

CHAPTER 1

What are we to do? Most certainly not nothing! Nothing has been done for far too long. We've inherited problems that started long ago; problems that stem from people doing nothing. The only difference in us and the ones before us, is our burdens have become so heavy that if we don't shake them, they are going to destroy us all; it will be our own damned fault for standing idly by, knowing but not wanting to know, seeing but not believing, and hearing but not understanding. We must do something because the only way evil overcomes good is when good doesn't stand up. The only way the darkness overcomes the light is when the light decides not to shine. I'm here to draw a line and you are going to have to choose a side.

Jesus said, "You are neither hot nor cold, but lukewarm, and therefore I will spew you from my mouth." That is the point we've once again reached in our world. I, myself, have too been guilty of staying out of the way, of wanting to speak but remaining quiet, and seeing but failing to acknowledge, but those days are gone for me. I've tried living the way society wants me to live, in the light while keeping my secrets in the shadows, but apparently that's not what was meant for me. Therefore, I risk all I have left and have chosen to fight with all I can at this point. These very words you're reading now are all the ammunition I have, and I'm using it as fast as it comes to me. Words aren't dangerous? I beg to differ. I'm far from the first or only person to know, think, or speak like this, but how many have written it? Have you ever wondered why?

The truth is dangerous, that's why, but it's my destiny to bring it to you, no matter the cost. I've gone through hell to have my eyes opened, because no one has had the balls to write about what's really going on. Therefore, I write in the hopes that you can read instead of experiencing. I've seen men killed over ramen noodles. I've seen men wearing badges lie to a judge and be believed because of the uniform they had on. I've been taken to jail and lost everything except my life and loved ones because of lies and greed, all to be able to see and tell you the truth. And it's that very truth that makes me unafraid of death or anything else man can do to me.

So, you see I've chosen my side, now it's time for you to do the same. Freedom or oppression, truth or lies, cowardice or bravery, and good or evil. The fight is real, the struggle is real, and once you know you can't unknow, so we must devise a plan to tear down what stands in order to create our perfect world. Our whole lives we've been manipulated, lied to, and used. These are the same tricks power-hungry men have used to lord over innocent people for centuries. It's simply evil seeds sown into men by the devil, and the fruit is now all around us. Nation against nation, religion against religion, and race against race. All manipulative strategies to keep the people of the world divided in order to keep the rulers of the world united, eating the fruit of our labors, telling us to obey the laws they create while they themselves do whatever they please.

They've angered my God with their hypocrisy. They've used their God granted power to our hurt and their own gain and they've had ample opportunity to change, to repent, but instead they've hardened their hearts, clung to their lies, trusted in their wealth, and now their judgement has been passed. God's people have been preparing for years for something. They didn't know who they were stocking up their weapons and ammunition for, or what they'd been building up massive amounts of wealth for, but now the time has come when all will be revealed, and The Lord's Army will need its resources.

Did you know that the men who founded America spent some of their own fortunes to fund the war? Although it was founded by hypocrites who created a country for free men that owned slaves (which makes absolutely no sense), and obviously shows that it was doomed from the very beginning. That's not the point right now though; the point is they believed in something better than what they had, something they couldn't see, something that didn't exist, and yet their faith in that compelled them to give their lives, their wealth, and even their sons to the cause. If they are to be considered great men, it's for their faith in an idea that hadn't yet manifested, not in founding this major problem we call a government today. Don't think we can accomplish anything without giving as much.

All will be called to give what they can for the cause. And the cause is this, a world in which all people are free to do what they do, as long as they don't harm anymore by doing so. A world in which everyone has a place to be who they are, instead of being what huge governments have brain washed them into being. A perfect world. God has granted me with the message and ability to write, but don't think that's all I'll give. I vowed a vow to surrender to my creator's will, and ever since the words have flowed like water. Now, I'm risking all I have left, which is myself, for this. You see, the inspiration was from God, the inspiration became a thought, the thought became words, the words are becoming a book, and it's up to us for the book to become reality. And that is how the word is manifested in the world.

CHAPTER 2

Before we go any further, I feel it is necessary to rid you of any doubts, increasing your faith by proving to you that this has been ordained in Heaven since the beginning, and to help confirm what your heart is whispering to you. We must all learn to listen to our heart and use that voice of God to overcome the doubts that the world has sown into our minds. Let us go to The Book of Daniel in the King James Version of The Holy Bible, chapter 2 verses 31 through 45.

31"Thou, O King, sawest, and behold a great image. This great image, whose brightness was excellent, stood before thee; and the form thereof was terrible. 32 This image's head was of fine gold, his breast, and arms full of silver, his belly and thighs of brass, 33 his legs of iron, his feet part iron and part clay. 34 Thou sawest till that a stone was cut out without hands, which smote the image upon his feet that were of iron and clay and broke them to pieces. 35 Then was the iron, the clay, the brass, the silver, and the gold, broken to pieces together, and became like the chaff of the summer threshing floors; and the wind carried them away, that no place was found for them: and the stone that smote the images became a great mountain and filled the whole earth.

36This is the dream; and we will tell the interpretation thereof before the king. 37Thou, O King, art a king of kings: for the God of heaven hath given thee a kingdom, power, and strength, and glory. 38And wheresoever the children of men dwell, the beasts of the field and the fowls of the heaven hath he given into thine hand, and hath made thee ruler over them all. Thou art this head of gold. 39And after thee shall arise another kingdom inferior to thee, and another third kingdom of brass, which shall bear rule over all the earth. 40And the fourth kingdom shall be strong as iron, forasmuch as iron breaketh in pieces and subdueth all things, and as iron that breaketh all these, shall it break in pieces and bruise." 41And whereas thou sawest the feet and toes, part potter's clay, and part iron, the kingdom shall be divided; but there shall be in it of the strength of iron, forasmuch as thou sawest the iron mixed with miry clay. 42And as the toes of the feet were part iron, and part clay, so the kingdom shall be partly strong, and partly broken

43And whereas thou sawest iron mixed with miry clay, they shall mingle themselves with the seed of men, but they shall not cleave one to another, even as iron is not mixed with clay. 44And in the days of these kings shall the God of heaven set up a kingdom, which shall never be destroyed, and the kingdom shall not be left to other people, but it shall break in pieces and consume all these kingdoms, and it shall stand for ever. 45Forasmuch as thou sawest that the stone was cut out of the mountain without hands, and that it breaks in pieces the iron, the brass, the clay, the silver and the gold; the great God hath made known to the king what shall come to pass hereafter, and the dream is certain, and the interpretation thereof sure.

So, let's think about this dream king Nebuchadnezzar had that the man of God, Daniel, interpreted. One of the key points we learn is that God will at some point set up a kingdom that will never be destroyed and will stand forever. This should increase your faith in our cause, but if you need more proof to believe the time has come, let's dive deeper into the dream and its interpretation.

We know from the scripture that a final kingdom

must fall before God establishes the one that lasts forever. This kingdom that must fall will be partly strong, and partly broken; it will be a kingdom that mingles the seeds of men. Does this sound familiar? It should. Tell me one kingdom in the history of the world made up of as many different types of people as America. Tell me one that has ever been as strong as far as military standards are concerned, but so divided within itself that its people are ready to tear it apart from the inside out. Name one in which the seeds of men have been intermingled as much as in America.

This country has every race of people in the world, and television has done its best to intermingle them all. Many have crossed the lines, but very few have remained together. Just as iron and clay don't cleave to one another. That's bullshit, you say; I don't have a problem with anyone who looks different than me, you say. Well, that's not what the scriptures are saying. It's saying they won't mix. Take a step back and look at your neighborhood. I bet it's predominantly one race. Zoom out a little more and look at a city, each section is predominantly one or the other. It's entirely natural to congregate towards people who look like you. We have eyes for a reason. The point is that although we all share the same language and land, we naturally separate ourselves. So, all the different types of Americans are not cleaving to one another.

So, when thinking about things from that perspective, it seems obvious that America is the kingdom that must fall before God sets up one that will last forever; one that shall never be destroyed. This is good news. It's also key to note that scripture doesn't say that the kingdom that God will establish will rule. It doesn't say rule because no one is meant to rule over anyone else. Free people do not have a ruler. We all know right from wrong, and only our own conscience should rule us. Hence, do as you do, just don't harm anyone while doing you.

When the children of Israel cried out to Samuel for a king, he was distraught. They had no king at the time, except God. This disheartened Samuel, so he turned to God for relief. God told him to give them what they wanted, and that it wasn't Samuel they were rejecting, but God. God told the prophet to warn the people; telling them a king would take their farms, tax their goods, and use their sons as soldiers. They still wanted their king, so they chose a man over God. It's the same question, but in reverse, that I ask of you today.

Do you really need people to tell you how to live your life? I damn sure don't! Do you need someone to take a third of your paycheck every week and spend it on causes you don't support, or give a fuck about? That sounds like extortion to me. Do you need a sumbitch to write more laws for you to follow every single year? I don't. Do you really need a government to tell you lies on a daily basis, keep secrets from you, and take care of you like you are some kind of fucking child? I don't; and if you do, I pity you.

If you so happen to be one of the latter, all I can say is, "O ye of little faith." Jesus said it long ago, and I feel his pain. The sorrow he had for people who would only believe if they saw, the grief he felt for people who were slaves and didn't even know it, and the anger he felt towards those who used the people's weaknesses against them for their own profit. The game they played hasn't changed. All that's changed is the names and the faces of those who play it. It's not a fucking game to me though, its life; and as far as I know it's the only life we get here on this earth. Why should we spend the only life we get working only to have to work some more, believing that someone else knows what's best for us, being who society taught us to be instead of who we truly are? Tell me why we shouldn't destroy America and every other government in the world. Better yet, tell me why God wouldn't want to. I don't believe you can.

One more detail we learn from king Nebuchadnezzar's dream and Daniels's interpretation, is that the stone that destroys the kingdom will be cut from a mountain, but not with human hands. If not by human hands, it must be by the hand of God! This tells me the way America is destroyed won't be in the conventional ways we think of. We are thinking of war in human terms. God's ways are higher than our ways, and therefore what He has planned, we won't know, until it's unveiled. I do know we will all have a part to play in it; I'm just not exactly sure what it is. We can learn from history how God has won battles, humbled the proud, and even wiped all trace of some people from the face of the earth. Sometimes with just a handful of men, and other times with whole armies of brave soldiers fighting for God. The strongest of nations have crumbled, walls have fallen at the sound of trumpets, and seas have closed in on the heathen. So, as you can clearly see, men do have a place in The Lord's Army.

I despise nothing more than people who rely only on the Lord and refuse to do anything themselves. Give me one example of a time when God used a coward to do the will of our Creator. Never! Fear none, but God. Could God have parted the Red Sea if the Israelites had refused to make the Exodus from Egypt? You lack in understanding if you think God will do anything for you if you fail to do anything for yourself.

Back to how God will destroy America, I still can't say for sure. I hope it's peaceably, but if it takes bloodshed then so be it. It's my own personal opinion, that those in power will not quit what they've got going on until we pry it from their cold dead hands, and if that be the case, then so be it as well. Once again, we must play our part in order for God's will to be accomplished. So now I ask you; has your faith increased, or do you still not believe?

CHAPTER 3

If that didn't convince you that America is destined to fall, I doubt there is anything that will. That's fine though, opposition is to be expected; as I said earlier, I'm here to draw a line. If you're not with us, you are against us, and that's fine because the one who is with us is stronger than all of you.

I will attempt to win you over with one last method, before we move on to our part. Imagine, if you can, a world in which everyone has a place to be who they are. One in which you don't have to live under the rule of other's beliefs. One where you are free. The definition of freedom is the power or right to act, think, or speak as one wants without hindrance or restraint. So, now that we've learned what freedom is, that it's more than just a word to be tossed around freely, and actually means something, you should be coming to the realization that you are about as far from free as one can be. So, can you imagine a world where we are free?

That is the goal, and everyone who opposes must be an enemy of freedom, and if you're an enemy of freedom then you're an enemy of mine and an enemy of my God's! This kingdom that my God will create is one that doesn't rule but is established over the entire earth. Even God doesn't want to rule, we are supposed to rule over ourselves. If a person's heart and conscience tell them they aren't wrong, who are you to do so? A perfect world would be a world in which people don't judge others for being who they are. If God wanted to rule you, free will wouldn't exist. If you aren't harming anyone by doing what you do, why shouldn't you be able to do it? You can't because men long to rule over other men. It's a power rush! Now imagine if we didn't have that problem; what kind of world would that be?

It would be a world in which people have enough understanding to respect others who believe differently from them and aren't offended by it. One in which people aren't scared to say how they really feel. Once again, one in which people are free. If this group of people only want to live around people like themselves, let them. Don't be offended if they don't want you around. Instead of getting your little panties in a wad, go where you are welcomed. If you're gay and the preacher doesn't want to marry you to your same sex partner, don't be mad at him. That's his right to believe however he wants to believe. How are you going to be mad at him? If this city is only one type of religion and you don't follow the same faith as them, why would you want to live with them or feel some type of way if they don't want you around? Because your understanding is so small you can't think about anyone but yourself and your own feelings. That's why.

So, in our world, what the next person thinks doesn't mean anything to you. When you get to that point, you are beginning to taste freedom. In a perfect world, you don't care what the next person does, in that way you aren't imposing your will upon their ability to act, think, or speak as they so choose, because if you do that you are an oppressor and an enemy of freedom. If they aren't harming anyone, why should you care? You shouldn't, but you've been told what to believe by those who have risen to power over the years, and instead of asking yourself, you simply believe what you've been taught. Well, what if it was all a lie? What if you've been taught wrong? What if the whole world has been deceived? Before you say I'm crazy, read this from the King James version of The Holy

Bible.

'God standeth in the congregation of the mighty; he judgeth among the Gods. "How long will ye judge unjustly, and accept the persons of the wicked? Selah". 3Defend the poor and the fatherless: do justice to the afflicted and needy. 4Deliver the poor and needy: rid them out of the hand of the wicked. 5They know not, neither will they understand; they walk on in darkness: all the foundations of the earth are out of the course. 6I have said , ye are Gods; and all of you are children of the most high. 7But ye shall die like men and fall like one of the princes. 8Arise, O God, judge the earth; for thou shalt inherit all nations.'

The foundations of the earth are out of course! That means nothing is the way it's supposed to be, but that's not what you thought is it? Our world, our identities, and our lives were hijacked ages ago by greedy men who knew the truth but withheld it from people, men who will and have killed to keep secret their knowledge and their firm grip on the world. But guess what, there is a God in heaven who sees all, and that very God is using me to reveal what has been hidden. They've all gone astray and its finally time to make them pay for their sins.

I have said, ye are Gods; and all of you are children of the most high. I bet your preacher never told you that. Wonder why? Perhaps they've never read that PSALM before, I guess that would mean they've never read the book in its entirety. Or, perhaps, the preacher's college failed to speak on this particular PSALM. Or could it possibly be that they've read it but fail to believe it. O ye of little faith! It could also be the fact that those very words and that very scripture inspired Jesus into finding out who he really was, which in turn cost him his life. Therefore, they fear for theirs.

Point is, you don't know what you are truly capable of, and that's just the way the people who rule the world want it. They use manipulation and lies to keep you down, but I'm using inspiration and truth to lift you up. The world is all of ours, they've just figured out how to take the whole pie and keep us satisfied with the crumbs. Fuck that and fuck them. You are, you can, and we will.

The last verse in the PSALM is a prophecy. Thou shalt inherit all nations. Just as Daniels interpretation said the final kingdom to be set up on earth would be by God. God will inherit all the nations established by men once they crumble, and then finally will we have one over all the earth established by God. A nation established with no malice or ulterior motive in mind. Taking the world back from thieves who wear suits and power-hungry maniacs who wear badges and ask for your votes. God will establish a kingdom where his people are free from oppression and unneeded rulers. Make no mistake, the world was created perfect, but men have corrupted and defiled the whole of creation.

CHAPTER 4

Now we will move on to how we must execute our cause. If you don't believe by now, you may as well quit reading, as I won't say anything else to try and convince you. I hate to sound harsh, but my patience fails me at times, and it is especially so when it comes to unbelievers. If you are under the impression that things aren't the way they are, then you are walking in darkness, and even though I've shined a light in your life, you refuse to be led by it.

As far as building The Lord's Army goes, there are several factors we must consider and address. First and foremost, we must understand that we have an established enemy who will stop at nothing when it comes to preserving the evil empire, they serve. This means they will pick us off one by one every single chance they get. Some they will throw in prison, some they will persecute with lies and trumped-up charges, and others they will simply kill. All these are methods they've been using for centuries. They try to cut off the head and kill the body. This is why we must have God as the head. I'd like to see those bitches try and cut that off.

With God as our head and inspiration, the rest of our army has positions to be filled. That means those of you who were called need to step up and do your duty. All of you who had a feeling when you were a child that God wanted you to save the world, just as my boy sitting beside me and myself did, I'm telling you now that it was real, and I'm calling you out on it. It's time to use your God given talent for something other than yourselves. If your gift is leading, then learn to lead for God; if it's speaking, then begin speaking for God; If it's making money, make it for God; if you're a soldier, fight for The Lord's Army; if you've got soldiers, pick a side and inspire them to fight for a cause that really matters. When we all begin to do what we were meant to do, the pieces will begin falling into place.

Do you rappers know the power you truly have? Just the influence over young minds you have is enough to change the world. You've got enough money to supply your troops, but what are you doing with the talent God has given you? Please don't tell me you're wasting it on causing division amongst yourselves, or God forbid just rapping about it. Are you really about the words that come from your mouth? Is your enemy really the guys on the other side of town, or is it the one who tells us all we can't be who, or do what we want to do? Remember the old proverb that says, "The enemy of your enemy is your friend." I think we all know who the common enemy is.

Preachers, what are you preaching to your congregation? Are you calling out the wrong for wrong, or just telling folks what they want to hear in order to fill the offering plates? You know the scriptures just as I do, is what I've been saying false? Does it seem I'm scared to say what needs to be said? Why should I fear death when my soul is immortal? If the soul is what gives life and the soul never dies, death is a deception! You, of all people, are supposed to know and preach the truth; why don't you speak on what's going on in the world today? Why say the things said before you repeatedly? Speak from the heart on matters that we are feeling today. In the spiritual and physical realms, we are in an age-long battle. God's soldiers aren't supposed to cower down or sit by when evil is constantly growing stronger and stronger.

To all the military men scattered across this country, I know you are ready and preparing for a civil war, but I want you to think bigger than that. Think of a revolution, a worldwide revolution! First off, there is no such thing as a "civil war." War is not civil. The objective of a war is to destroy your enemy by any means necessary. The word civil has no place in war. I've had the same feeling for years that you have. The feeling that something is coming, the feeling that I need to be ready for whatever, the feeling that war is brewing. Well guess what, it is. Everyone feels it, most just refuse to acknowledge it. You're not wrong, and you're not crazy. You've listened to the spirit inside of you, and the world has tried to condemn you for it. I'm here to praise you, because anyone led by their spirit is led by God, and anyone led by God is a friend of mine.

To every black, white, brown, yellow and mixed person on this earth who has a heart and soul and knows something isn't right, and who is tired of being treated like no one; I am here to tell you that you are someone and no one person is higher than the next. We are the body of God with the creator as the head.

The evil ones of the world are no more than a handful, but at this very moment their evil hand is clasped around our neck and is slowly, but steadily, tightening its grip. They want so desperately to separate us from our God because they know that it is the only way they can win. The eye of God sees first the evil grip, then the neck feels it, and if the black hand and white hand don't quit squabbling with one another long enough to feel their own neck, we will all be destroyed together. I see the evil and I feel the grip and I am telling you to put aside your differences and release this evil grip from our throat. Be forewarned, if you don't, we won't be here much longer.

If we as people can't shake the evil from our world, powers greater than us will accomplish what we failed to do. Why would we be worth saving if we couldn't even save ourselves? Why would we be worth saving if we wouldn't save ourselves? Why would they who are stronger than us not destroy us along with evil? The governments of the world and anyone who represents or is a part of them are slowly destroying our earth, robbing the people, and keeping vulnerable truths out of our hands, and they think it's okay to do as they are told when their hearts tell them it's wrong. If that isn't lost, I don't know what is. If it's lost, it's our duty to press forward and start afresh.

CHAPTER 5

Your eyes see the signs, your minds try and comprehend, but you refuse to understand with your heart. We see lights toying with the military on a regular basis, but you still refuse to believe. When a nation goes to war, all you hear them speak of is their military might and supporting allies. Never once trusting in God as their strength or protector. Even Israel, who is currently at war in Gaza, has not mentioned God one time in any news broadcast I've seen. You'd think they would know from their own history, that anytime their nation trusted in anything other than God, ruin lied ahead. Ponder on this scription from the King James version of The Holy Bible. Isaiah chapter 6, 8 through 10. 8Also, I heard the voice of the Lord, saying, whom shall I send, and who will go for us? Then said I, here am I; send me. 9And he said, Go, and tell this people, hear ye indeed, but understand not; and see ye indeed, but perceive not. 10Make the heart of this people fat, and make their ears heavy, and shut their eyes; lest they see with their eyes, and hear with their ears, and understand with their heart, and convert and be healed.

Jesus quoted the same scripture concerning the people of his time, and it saddens me to quote it concerning the people of mine. Our technology has progressed, but we are none the wiser. It may be because a limit was placed on what we can know, or it may be simply arrogance and pride that is holding us back. I know that today wisdom and folly still exist just as in King Solomon's time, and I know that there are still those who see and hear but fail to understand, just as in Isaiah and Jesus' time. So, are we really that more advanced than our ancestors? Hell no!

As far as seeing the signs of the times go, let us talk about the lights that have been seen in the sky by militaries and civilians alike in nations all across the world. Once again, we can use scriptures to confirm that these are beings made of light. Moses and seventy of Israel's elders saw the light of God on the mountain; Elijah was taken into Heaven by a whirlwind to a chariot of fire waiting; Elisha prayed that God would open his servants eyes, and when he did, he saw heavens army of beings made of fire; Jesus was transfigured on the mount into light; the wise men followed a star to the place Jesus was born, and the list goes on. The point is that beings of light or fire have been around since or before us. They are part of The Lord's Army as well, and I've got a feeling they are appearing more and more as a warning to us. You are either a child of light or a child of darkness, and it's up to you to choose which.

I must warn you though, of one of the dark side tactics. It pretends it is good as the light side. It uses deception and lies to convince those with no understanding that the soldiers of light in the world are really evil men. No way, you say. On the contrary, I say. The court systems and governments of men have prosecuted men and women of God since the beginning of time. All for being different, calling them out on their evil, and living free from the bond's civilizations have put on men. Then after they are dead, you praise them, label them as saints, and regret your evil deeds. This very reason is why it's said, "that of all people ten percent have heavenly knowledge, and of these ten percent, only half will share what they know," because it falls on deaf ears, you want to kill them for their words, and at times it seems as no use to tell you anyways.

I'm not speaking in parables, riddles, or allegories. My words are clear, and my message is precise. God has sent countless prophets and wise men before me, who only spoke to those seeking, but I'm speaking to everyone. Even a child should be able to understand my words.

I explained the injustice that goes on in our courtrooms, I've told you how "good guys" are really bad, I've said that you are all Gods and children of the most high, and most of all I've told you we can. Now it's up to all of you to open your eyes and see or continue to walk on in darkness. Come to the light and be a child of God or continue on your path and die like men. Stand up for a cause greater than yourself or continue on working for nothing but self.

Let me share one last thing before we move on. Once you understand that the kingdom of God dwells within you; allow the spirit of God to lead you and allow the spirit of God to use you for God's will; you will be moving toward holiness, and holiness is nothing more than becoming a whole being. Not one in which the flesh and spirit war with one another, but one that lets the spirit guide the flesh. It's in this spirit that we gain eternal life. The spirit is our energy source, it's what makes us, and it's what determines our fate. Light and darkness both contain energy, and the choice is yours alone to decide which one drives you. As soon as I made a vow to God, the whole purpose of my life slowly began to change. The course in which I was handed slowly but constantly altered. I've been a drug dealer, a plumber, an offshore oilfield hand, a pipeline worker, a mechanic, and then God turned me into a writer. I didn't go to college and I despised school, but here I am writing words like you've never read. How can it be any other than the Spirit of God inside of me? How could those jobs have ever led me to this? They couldn't, and wouldn't have, it's only when I finally quit thinking with my mind and started listening to the voice of God inside my heart that I was led to my true purpose in life. I'm not special, I'm no different than anyone else, so if God can use me, God can use you. Anything is possible to those who believe, and that's all you have to do.

The Lord's Army

CHAPTER 6

Now, we will proceed on to our mission. If you haven't noticed yet, I'm not keeping this a secret, we aren't whispering it in bunkers, and nothing is based on deception. This is to show the power of God. We are going to tell them openly what our plan is, just to show that Heaven rules over earth and God's will cannot be stopped. Where do they do that at? Only in The Lord's Army.

The concept is quite simple, actually. All we've got to do is stick together. We must be armed because arms are the great equalizer. We must have supplies, and we must not compromise. We can't deal with the politicians or leaders of this God forsaken government whatsoever. That would be playing their game with them, and we aren't here to play games. They can either quit and walk away or face their fate.

The question you must ask yourself is, what is it God can use me for? Then you will know your place in the cause. If you're still reading, you must believe. So, from here on out, I'm only speaking to believers. Brothers and sisters, those who see the truth, we must pool our resources and begin something great.

If you've got money, buy a couple old army trucks off an online government auction instead of that new corvette. If you're not a convicted felon; buy guns and ammo for those who can't. If you are a natural born leader, lead those who will listen. If you are a solider, be a solider for God. Why give to a church who already was the biggest building on the block, but won't even let the homeless sleep in the pews at night? That isn't a true house of God. Why horde money, when politicians have inflated our dollar so much that its barely worth wiping your ass with? If they aren't stopped, their greed is going to starve us all to death. What will your almighty dollar be worth when you can't even buy food with it? Not a damn thing, just like it was during the depression. This country is teetering on the verge of destruction and all we have to do is give it a little push to help it fall.

What will we do if that happens? We will get up in the morning and do what we always do. We make the world; they just skim off the top. It's simple; if you drive, you pay a road tax; if you have children, you pay a school tax; if you go to the doctors; you pay your bill and so on. Without different governments, we no longer have wars of nation against nation, freeing up billions of your dollars, that are used for death. Would 9/11 have happened if the American government hadn't been meddling in affairs that were none of its concern for years beforehand? No, it wouldn't have! This country has plundered the resources of the world, exploiting the people, and you wonder why we are despised?

The truth of the matter is that this government has exploited its people as well, and that's what I want people all across the globe to know. It's not the people of America that you should hate, it's the government. Perhaps some blame should fall on us, the people, for allowing them to get this out of control, but they've been like a tumor that grows without being seen or felt until it's almost too late. To those who have been wronged, to those our government has imposed its will over, and to those who've grown to hate us; I apologize for our lack of keeping this monster in check. It was our duty from the beginning to keep their power in check, and at that we the people have utterly failed, and for that, I am truly sorry.

I can tell you that most all the people, although blind to most facts, do sense something has gone majorly wrong. This government is no longer for the people, and by the people. It's slowly alienated itself from its people by not having term limits, generations of the same vile creatures wearing suits and telling lies, and the lure of power causing them to write law after law after law. It is now them versus us, and once again I'll say, "The enemy of my enemy, is my friend," and the American government is the common enemy.

So, back to my fellow countrymen, we do have the power, they just don't want us to know it. To prove this point, I'm going to give you two examples. One, I was a part of and the other I had no clue what was happening, but I reaped the benefits of it.

The first happened while I was in federal prison for exercising my second amendment right to bear arms. While serving a sixty-month sentence for being a felon in possession of a firearm, we got a new warden over the compound. This new warden, high on his power over other men, decided he was going to implement some new rules, such as not turning the televisions on until 10:00 AM instead of 5:00 AM, forcing us to wear our khaki uniforms while inside the unit, and a couple more meaningless, bullshit ass rules. Well, what this fool failed to realize is that, whereas he goes home every night, this place was our home. What he also failed to realize was that we had a lot more people than he did. Eighteen hundred, to be exact, lived in that facility.

So, as the one hundred or so correction officers began to implement their new rules, we began to whisper and grumble amongst ourselves. The whispers became open conversations, and the conversations became a movement. Eventually the different races all put aside their differences and came together for the greater good of all. A plan was devised, and a list of demands were typed up, copied, and distributed. On the day set forth we were all to stay in our units, turn down our meals, and keep from all our slavely duties. Those who had money, stocked up on noodles to feed those who had none, those who were scared and wanted to cross the line like good little inmates were deterred by strength, and on that day we all stood together.

To say that we had the government spooked that

day, would be to say the least. They sent in their SIS division to negotiate a deal with us, which is why I say we can't negotiate with them now, and their first offer we turned down. That ended the first day and we were left all alone that night. The one guard who usually slept in their office between the two – one hundred-and fifty-man zones didn't even come in. So, there we were, three - two story buildings, full of pissed off convicts who've learned to hate the government they were born into, left to our own devices. It was fun and felt special to us all. They watched us on the cameras, of course, but what could they do? Our strength lies in numbers.

We ate together, set shit on fire together, and let them motherfuckers know who really runs shit, together! They did not like it, but we loved it. Day two of the strike brought more negotiations, all we wanted was for things to stay the way they were, but that just seemed too much. Once again, negotiations were broken off and we were left all alone. Now, keep in mind this place was surrounded by guard towers with armed guards. They had tear gas, riot gear, and anything else at their disposal, but they didn't have the troops we had. We were fighting for what we believed in, and they were fighting for money, and there lies a huge difference between the two. Is it any wonder to you now, that American troops have fought for twenty years in the middle east, only to leave with nothing done, but more hatred bred, and its own veterans cursed with mental illnesses because they fought a fight only to find out they didn't believe in it. The greatest military might the word has ever known couldn't destroy a group of men who believed in their cause and fought with outdated weapons and improvised explosives! I wonder why?

Back to the narrative. So, the third day arrived and to our surprise, the federal correctional officers agreed to let things be the way they were before the new warden came in. We had won! The strike was over! Things would remain the same! Wrong, they told us what we wanted to hear and kept their word only long enough to let the movement lose its momentum. As soon as we'd thought we won, we all parted ways. Race back with race and gang with gang. This was when they slowly began to implement their strategy and little by little impose the new rules.

All was not done in vain, because although we won one battle but slowly lost the next few, I learned their game. I also learned from our mistakes and now I'm giving it all to you. Our first mistake was believing the words that flowed from their deceptive lips. Second, we disbanded, and all went our separate ways, proving the old parable "Divide your enemies in order to conquer" true. And lastly, but least of all, we did not utterly destroy our enemy when we had the chance.

The second incident occurred at this very facility I'm currently being held against my will in. This food is by far the worst here out of all the places I've ever been. Put it like this, the woman over the kitchen (who claims to be a Christian), brags about how she has costs down to a little over two dollars a day to feed each inmate. So, as you can imagine, the food isn't worth a fuck! Being that this is a regional facility, it houses pre-trial state and federal inmates, county trustees (such as myself), and state convicts. The state pays this county so many dollars per day for each convict, the feds pay for each federal inmate awaiting trial, and I'm certain they get money off of us county inmates as well. So, just as in any business, the lower the cost, the more the profit. Which is why the food doesn't have cheese in the macaroni, sugar in the oatmeal, salt in the grits, and we only get one slice of cheese with four pieces of bread and two slices of bologna for dinner.

Apparently, the twenty or so guys in the federal pod had enough of the shit, so they all got together and went on a food strike. The officers brought the trays in, and they pushed them right back out the door. Now being that this whole operation is about money, and the jail didn't want to lose their contract with the feds, the menu suddenly changed. Don't think we are getting steaks, but we now get chicken once a week instead of once every two months, and now they put cheese in the macaroni. They even started giving three baby carrots with a slice of celery, but unfortunately, we are now back to two carrots a day.

Point is twenty men bonded together and made a difference. Of course, it won't last forever because evil never ceases, but it did happen, and it did have an impact. It proves our strength when we stand together. It proves that when out gunned and locked in a cage, we still have power. It proves that we can if we want to.

So, let's take these examples and see how they can be applied to the world. I happen to know that here in my county there are only eighty-four deputies including the sheriff. There are some reserves and jailers as well and if we include them, we will put their numbers up to a very liberal two hundred. Now, if you include the city cops from the two cities in this county, we will put their total up to around five hundred. Then we will add in the department of corrections officers and the investigators that work for the state attorney's office and we will bump their number up to six hundred. Lastly, but certainly not least, since we have a federal building, we will count all the federal officers ranging from bailiffs to drug and firearm agents, and we will settle on a very liberal one-thousand-armed agents of the machine in my county.

On the flipside of that, we have the people. Fifty thousand people would be a very very conservative number concerning the people who live in my county. Of that number, let's say half want to live in their little shell and pretend like nothing's going on. But the other half, on the other hand, have been slowly but surely seeing things. They've grown to distrust their government, they have to cheat on their taxes just to make it, they know the struggle is real! Tell me how those one-thousand paid soldiers could withstand twenty-five thousand people with a cause. They can't, that's how.

Every man in my family own guns. Guns with an "s" that is, and every single one of them believes a civil war will come. When I was on a job eighteen years ago, the electricians, carpenters, AC guys, and plumbers like me talked shit about fishing, hunting, parties the weekend before, and getting paid on Friday. Never was politics, civil war, or the dollar not being worth anything ever spoken of, but in the past three years those topics were talked about every single day and dominated the conversation of the day. So, I know what's being talked about when people are amongst those they trust, and as we've learned before, a thought becomes a word, word's become conversation, and eventually conversation will become reality. So, now you know you're not alone in feeling this way; there are more with us than there are with them.

Before we move on to the next chapter, I do need to mention that to some, if not many, of those listed earlier that are a part of the kingdom that must fall will desert their paid positions and join us. I've heard it directly from their own mouths. All I have to say to them is, you better do it before the line is drawn. Being that for so long you have been the ones executing someone else's will and therefore a major part of the problem, you will only have one opportunity to choose the right side. So, choose quickly and choose wisely.

CHAPTER 7

We know that this country is destined to fall, we know God is on our side, and we know that we vastly outnumber our enemy. Now we should examine the enemy close, in order to identify their flaws and exploit them. Of all the law officers who've been real enough to open up to me, half of them admitted that when they first began their careers, it was for a noble cause. They believed they were joining the fight against evil. They were following the dream they had as a child, but once on the streets, they slowly began to realize things weren't quite what they had thought they were. This is easily explained. Long ago, they began to "fight fire with fire," but little did they know though, that this tactic would be the beginning of their end. It's once again, another trick from the Devil's playbook, and they are too blind to realize it. Substitute the word 'fire' with the word 'evil', and you now have "fight evil with evil." First off, good does no evil, so if the good guys do evil, they are in fact evil, and no longer good. Secondly, if evil fights evil, all you have is evil. And lastly, since evil is dark and deceptive, all consumed by it think they are good, but how can one see through the darkness?

So, what you now have are men with badges, who, as they've matured, have begun to lose faith in their cause. This is a great thing. It sucks for them as what's on their conscious is between them and God, but it's beautiful for us. Of course, I hope they repent, but at the end of the day, it's their souls in jeopardy, not mine. Men who don't believe in their cause have, all throughout history, fled when faced with eminent defeat, so all we must do is show up and show them. They think they can beat, kill, steal, and take time from people without any consequences because the law, written by just as vile creatures as themselves, says they can. Well, if they get to do what the words written on paper say they can do, why can't we? Now we have words on paper just as they do, and these are even more powerful. "It ain't no fun when the rabbits got the gun" is it? Or in this instance, when I've got the pen.

Their words use trickery and deception to control men. Mine are the truth. Now which is good, and which is evil? These questions I've been presenting you with are all to free your mind from the bondage under which this society had placed you under. They want you to do and believe as you are told; all I want is for you to be who you are, know what and why you believe what you believe, and to be free. So, when they condemn my words and try to suppress my writing, know that it's because they don't want you to be free. They don't want you to think. They want to control you, just as they always have.

CHAPTER 8

So, we talk about taking our world back. We accept all those who see the light, recognize the truth, and leave their oppression behind. We stock up on weapons, ammunition, and all other supplies needed for war. And then, we unite and execute our plan. We try it peacefully, but if they refuse to relinquish their power, we take it from them by force. We utterly destroy the establishment in the name of God and start afresh. We create a perfect world, and then we return to our labors, which make us a civilization. It can happen that easily if you just have faith!

The scripture tells us we are Gods but shall die like men. That's because God's children are only meant to be ruled over by God. Evil men have placed a yolk on you that you must shake in order to be who you were created to be. Learn to live free and say, "fuck this society!"

www.ingramcontent.com/pod-product-compliance
Lightning Source LLC
Chambersburg PA
CBHW051557120626
46551CB00013B/1559